Star Spangled Flag Window Hanger

★ **Designed by Paula and Kenneth Moliver**

Paint a stylized flag on silk to hang in your window.

You Will Need

12″ round silk window decoration*
Silk paint*: red, blue, black
Gutta*: colorless, black
Paintbrush*
Coarse pretzel salt
12″ length of 1/8″ satin ribbon: red, white, blue
Embroidery needle, pencil

* Used in this project: Janlynn for ARTY'S silk hanging • Pebeo Setasilk paint: Hermes Red, Gitane Blue; Gutta • Robert Simmons round #6 paintbrush.

Instructions

1 Place design under silk and trace pole and red stripes, using pencil. Remove paper design.

2 Paint flagpole with black gutta. Mix equal 7mm drops of colorless gutta and red paint. Paint stripes with red mixture. Mix blue paint in same way and paint stars. Let dry.

3 For crystal pattern background, dilute one part blue paint to three parts water, as background. Paint background. Sprinkle salt immediately on background while still wet. As paint dries, the salt will push paint. When paint is dry remove salt.

4 Thread ribbons together through silk with an embroidery needle. Knot ends and hang in window.

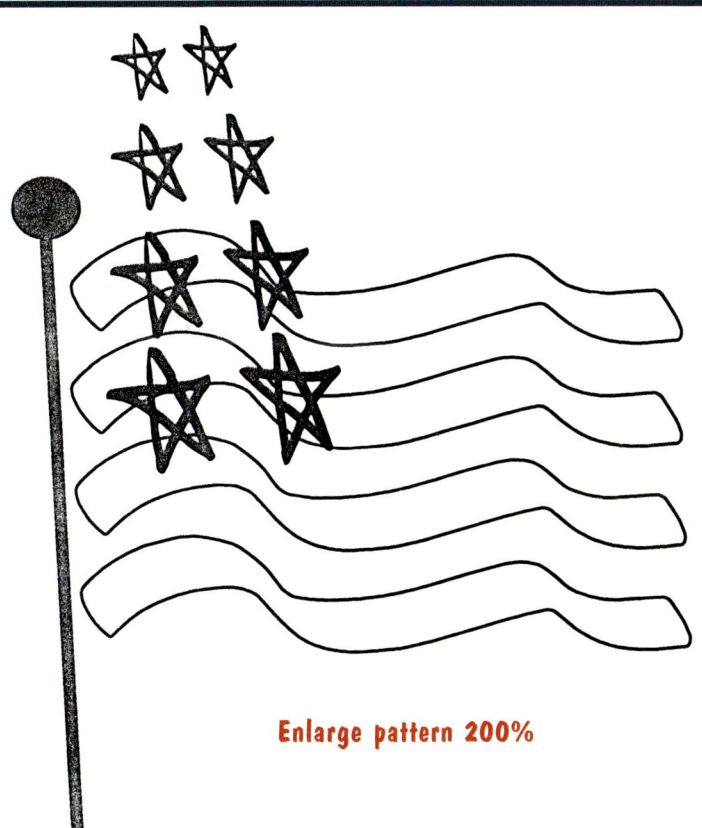

Enlarge pattern 200%

HURON PUBLIC LIBRARY
333 WILLIAMS STREET
HURON, OHIO 44839

Star Candle

★ **Designed by Koren Russell**

Thin wire adds sparkle to these patriotic stars. When your candle burns low, simply remove the star wrap from the old candle and place it around a new one.

You Will Need

3¾″ x 4¾″ white candle
5″ diameter wood base
Four 1″ wood balls
Five 2⅜″ wood stars
14 brass 7mm jump rings
8 yd. 34-gauge brass wire
Acrylic paint*: red, white, beige
Drill with 1/16″ bit
Paintbrushes, pencil, ruler, scissors, needle-nose pliers, wire snips

*Used in this project: DecoArt Americana acrylic paint: Deep Burgundy, Admiral Blue, Toffee.

Instructions

1 Drill hole through left and right points of each star, 1/16″ in from edge.

2 Draw horizontal line 1⅛″ down from top of one star. Below line, pencil in ¼″ wide vertical stripes. Paint area above stripes blue. Paint edges and backs of stars blue. Paint beige stars in blue area. Paint alternating red and beige stripes.

3 Cut 40″ piece of wire. Wrap wire randomly around star, beginning and ending on backside. Twist wire ends together. Trim wire ends.

4 Separate ends of two jump rings. (See Figure 1 on page 11.) Insert one ring through each hole. Squeeze ends together. Join five stars by adding a jump ring between rings on points of stars. Loop wire through rings on end stars four times. Twist ends of wire together. Trim wire ends.

5 Paint base blue and wood balls red. Wrap two yards of wire around base, beginning and ending on backside. Twist wire ends together. Trim wire ends. Evenly space and glue balls on bottom of base.

What If You . . .

Use individual stars as pins or magnets. They would also make great ornaments. Just drill one hole through the top point of star and insert a jump ring. Hang with a gold cord.

Polymer Clay Patriotic Pen

★ Designed by Ginny Baker

Write letters in style with this bright clay-covered pen.

You Will Need

2 oz. package polymer clay*: red, white, blue
One Bic Round Stic Pen
⅜″ star pattern cutter*
Baby wipes, baking pan, craft knife, needle tool, pliers, rolling pin or brayer, waxed paper, paper

* Used in this project: Amaco Fimo Soft clay: Metallic Red, Metallic Blue, White
  • Kemper star cutter.

Wash hands well before beginning. Baby wipes are useful for cleaning hands between clay colors (especially red and blue) and to clean rolling pin or brayer. Do not use tools with food after using with clay.

Instructions

1 Remove ink cartridge from pen using pliers. Do not remove tip. Set ink cartridge aside.

2 Use hands and brayer to condition (soften) clay. Roll five uniform ⅛″ ropes of white clay and five ropes of red clay, slightly longer than length of pen. Alternate colors and lay ropes side by side on waxed paper, beginning with white and ending with red. Press ropes gently against one another.

3 Using rolling pin, roll across ropes several times until flattened into striped sheet with no seams. Clean pin between rolls.

4 Trim one edge of clay sheet straight. Lay pen along this edge. Trim sheet to extend ¼″ longer than pen at each end. Roll clay sheet around pen. Trim away clay so edges butt together neatly and do not overlap. Stripe colors should alternate at seam. Roll pen gently to blend and remove seam line. Trim away clay from tip and top of pen. Press and smooth top end so it is rounded.

5 Lay one-quarter package of blue clay on waxed paper and flatten to ³⁄₁₆″ thick. Cut a 1¼″ x 2-¼″ piece. Lay pen on piece so ¼″ of clay extends beyond end of pen. Roll clay around pen until edges meet, trimming so edges butt together. Roll gently to smooth seam. Trim away clay at end of pen as before and smooth end. With needle tool, poke holes around bottom edge of blue piece for stitch marks.

6 Lay one-quarter package of white clay on waxed paper and flatten to ¹⁄₁₆″ thick. Cut out ten stars. Press stars randomly around blue top of pen.

7 Lay pen on piece of plain white paper in baking pan. Bake at 265° for 30 minutes. Remove from oven and cool completely before touching. Once cooled, re-insert ink cartridge.

Painted Clay Pot and Poke

★ Designed by Dianne Buscema-Gerogianis

Turn a plain clay pot and wood star into a colorful accent that will look great on a desk or windowsill.

You Will Need

Pot
3″ terra cotta pot
Acrylic paint*: red, navy blue, white
Acrylic paint, gold*
Gloss varnish*
Fine-point black permanent marker, paintbrushes*, pencil, sponge brush, toothbrush, tracing paper

* Used in this project: Delta Ceramcoat acrylic paints: Bright Red, Navy Blue, White; varnish • DecoArt metallic acrylic paint: Emperor's Gold • Loew-Cornell paintbrushes: #5 Round, #12 Flat.

Poke
2″ wood star*
3/4″ wood heart*
8″ length of 1/8″ wood dowel
Acrylic paint*: red, navy blue, white
Gloss varnish*
Craft glue, fine-point black permanent marker, paintbrush*, sponge brush, toothpick

* Used in this project: Lara's Crafts star; heart • Delta Ceramcoat acrylic paint: Bright Red, Navy Blue, White; varnish • Loew-Cornell paintbrush: #6 Flat Shader.

Instructions

Pot

1 Paint rim of pot two coats of white. Paint inside and bottom of pot navy blue. Trace star pattern and cut out. Trace stars onto pot and paint white. Paint diagonal 5/8″ wide stripes around rim red. Paint top of rim gold. Draw wiggly lines and slash marks along bottom of rim with black marker.

2 Dip toothbrush into white paint and spatter. Dip toothbrush in red paint and spatter. Let dry completely. Paint with a coat of varnish.

Poke

1 Paint star white. Let dry. Paint wavy 1/4″ wide stripe red. Paint heart navy blue. Let dry. Add dots, using toothpick and white. Glue heart in middle of star.

2 Paint dowel white. Glue star on dowel. Paint with coat of var-

Star

★★ 4 ★★

Birdhouse

★ Designed by Gigi Wright-Turpin

Paint a birdhouse and trim with small stars, curled wire, and raffia.

You Will Need

6″ tall birdhouse*
Acrylic paint*: white, Moroccan red, Barn red, Storm blue
Eight thin strands of 18″ long red raffia
Small bird
24″ of wire
Two small eyehooks
5/8″ wide transparent tape
2″ wide masking tape
Wood stars*: 11 medium, 5 small
Paintbrushes*

* Used in this project: Walnut Hollow birdhouse • Forster Woodsies stars • Eagle Brush Company Millennium Series paintbrushes: #725-5, Round, Flat Shader, Script Liner • Delta Ceramcoat paint.

Instructions

1 Paint roof blue. Paint house red.

2 Using transparent tape, mark off horizontal stripes on front, sides, and back of birdhouse, leaving 5/8″ between tape strips. Paint stripes white. Paint stitch lines on each stripe: white on red stripes; red on white stripes.

3 Place all stars on sticky side of masking tape. Paint stars white. With blue, paint stitch lines around each star.

4 With red, shade under roof (both sides) and around hole.

5 Glue five medium stars on each side of roof. Glue small bird on perch.

6 Screw one eyehook on each side of roof to attach wire. Curl one end of wire around a paintbrush and thread the rest through one eyehook. Curl middle area of wire. Thread remaining wire through other eyehook and curl end to hold.

7 Holding eight thin strands of raffia together, tie in a bow around top of wire. Glue medium star in center of bow and small stars on raffia ends.

Patriotic Foil Fames

★ **Designed by Lynda Scott Musante**

Place your favorite photos in shiny stars-and-stripes foil frames.

You Will Need

For Both
¼" wide double-sided tape*
Stylus*
Decorative-edge scissors*: deckle
Cardboard, craft knife, ruler, scissors
Two sheets blue foil*
One sheet each: silver, red foil*
One sheet silver star holographic stickers*

Single Frame
3½" x 5" Craft frame*

Double Frame
3½" x 6" Double craft frame*

*Used in this project: Reynolds Bright Ideas Ultra foil, stickers, frame, tape, stylus • Fiskars scissors.

Instructions

Single Frame

1 Cut a 6½" x 8½" rectangle of blue foil. Apply two 2" strips of double-sided tape on each corner on the back (silver) side of rectangle. Place frame right side up on table. Remove backing from eight pieces of tape. Center foil over the frame front and press foil in place. Smooth foil over frame and fold to back.

2 Turn frame over and place four 2" strips of tape along each edge of frame opening. Cut along dotted lines as shown in figure and fold flaps to back of frame. (Figure 1)

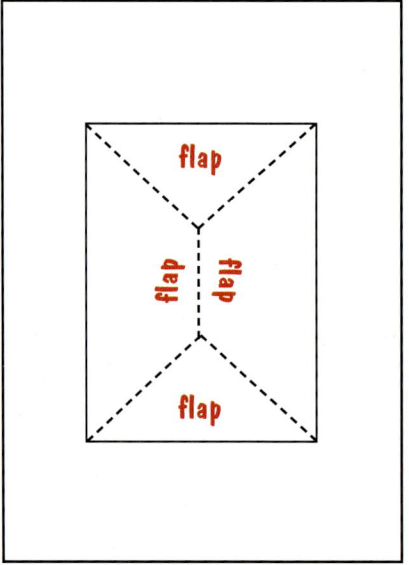

Figure 1

3 Cut two 3" x 3" x 4¼" triangles of silver foil. Trim 4¼" side of each triangle with decorative scissors. Place a strip of tape along edges of each triangle; remove the backing. Place one triangular piece over the upper right corner, having decorative edge touching corner of frame opening. Fold foil to back of frame. Repeat for bottom left corner. Cut two 1¾" x 1¾" x 2½" triangles of red foil. Trim 2½" side of each triangle with decorative scissors. Apply red triangles to frame in same way as silver triangles.

★★ 6 ★★

4 Adhere silver star stickers randomly on blue foil. Use the stylus to emboss (outline) around stars and along edge of red foil. Texture blue foil with a crosshatch pattern. (Figure 2)

Figure 2

5 To cover back of frame with blue foil, cut a 6″ x 8¼″ piece. Place tape along edges of foil; remove backing. Place foil on INSIDE of back frame. Fold foil to outside of frame. Place frame on blue foil and trace around it. Cut piece of foil slightly inside lines. Place tape along corners of foil in same way as before; remove backing. Place foil on frame back and press in place.

Double Frame

1 Cut a 3″ by 5″ rectangle of blue foil. Apply two 2″ strips of double-sided tape on each corner on the back (silver) side of rectangle. Place frame right side up on table. Remove backing from eight pieces of tape. Center foil over the frame front and press foil in place.

2 See Step 2 of Single Frame to cut and fold foil around frame openings.

3 Cut a 4½″ x 6½″ rectangle from silver foil. Place silver foil (shiny side down) on table. Use stylus to trace around outside of frame; open frame and trace around two frame openings. Cut a 4¾″ x 2⅝″ piece from paper. Center the paper over the two outlined openings on foil. Use stylus to trace around outside edge of paper. Use craft knife to cut out along these lines. Cut and apply a 2″ strip of tape along the top edge of frame front. Do not remove backing. Place silver foil in place so the larger opening is centered on the frame openings. Hold in place and remove the backing from the tape and rub foil to adhere. Apply a 2″ strip of tape along inside edge of each opening. Apply a 2″ strip of tape along bottom edge of frame front. Remove backings and press foil in place.

4 Turn frame over. Apply tape on foil that extends on three sides; remove backings. Smooth foil over frame and fold to back. Put a strip of tape along the upper edge of foil; remove backing and press foil down.

5 For stripes, place red foil on table with wrong (silver) side up. Place a strip of tape along the 12″ length of the sheet. Do not remove backing. Make a ¼″ wide strip by cutting along both edges of tape with decorative scissors. Begin at lower left corner, having ¼″ of stripe extending over frame edge. Peel backing a little at a time and press down stripe. Cut stripe ¼″ beyond right frame edge. Fold stripe ends to back of frame.

Add additional stripes in same way, cutting stripes even along inside silver edges.

6 Adhere silver star stickers randomly on blue foil. Use the stylus to emboss (outline) around stars and along edges of red foil.

7 To cover back of frame with blue foil, cut a 3¾″ x 6¼″ piece. Place tape along edges of foil; remove backing. Place foil on INSIDE of back frame. Fold foil to outside of frame. Place frame on blue foil and trace around it. Cut piece of foil slightly inside lines. Place tape along corners of foil in same way as before; remove backing. Place foil on frame back and press in place.

Ideas for Working With Foil

There are numerous products that can be used with foil. Most tools intended for scrapbooking and memory crafting, including punches, crimpers, and rubber stamps, work well with Ultra Foil. Further, such surface treatments as rub-on paint transfers, stickers, and some rubber stamp inks can be used to enhance the foil.

Plastic Canvas Flag Pin

★ Designed by Darla Fanton

You can stitch this lapel pin in a snap!

Color Key

- ☐ Blue
- ╲ Red
- ○ White
- ◇ White French knot: 1 strand, wrap once

You Will Need

15 x 13 hole piece of 10-mesh plastic canvas
2 yds. each pearl cotton*: blue, white, red
Size 22 tapestry needle
Needle, scissors, pin back or small safety pin, white sewing thread

* Used in this project: Anchor #5 pearl cotton: blue (149), white (2), red (46).

Note: See Stitching Guide on page 25.

Instructions

1 See Chart. Stitch flag, using two strands of pearl cotton and reverse continental stitch. At same time overcast with blue where appropriate, red and white at beginning and end of each stripe, and red along remaining top and bottom edges. With one strand of white, work French knots.

2 With sewing thread, whip-stitch pin back on wrong side of lapel pin.

Doily Angel Pin

★ Designed by Ann Butler

Make a guardian angel to watch over you.

You Will Need

2″ heart doily
¾″ wood plug head
9 Red 4mm beads
4″ of ⅛″ wide blue satin ribbon
¾″ pin back
Black permanent marker, glue*, needle, thread

* Used in this project: Crafter's Pick glue.

Instructions

1 With marker, draw eyes on head. For halo, thread six beads on thread. Glue one thread end on back of head. Wrap beads around front of head and glue other thread end on back of head. Glue head on doily.

2 Tie ribbon in bow and glue below head. Cut ends at a slant. Glue three beads on doily. Glue pin back on back of angel.

Flag Bookmark

★ Designed by Phyllis Dobbs

Cross-stitch on vinyl and embellish with strings of beads. This is a good project for a beginner!

You Will Need

14-count vinyl aida*, 1″ x 4½″
6-strand cotton embroidery floss*: red, white, blue
One pack each of seed beads*: red, white, blue
No. 24 tapestry needle
Beading needle
White beading thread
Scissors

* Used in this project: Charles Craft, Inc. aida • DMC embroidery floss: blanc, blue (825), red (321) • Mill Hill Glass seed beads: Red (02013), White (00479), Blue (00020).

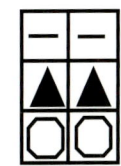

Color Key

– Blanc
▲ 825 Blue
☐ 321 Red

Instructions

1 Following chart, cross-stitch design with two strands of embroidery floss. Trim vinyl weave to two rows around edges of stitching so there is a row of empty aida holes all around flag.

2 Thread beading needle with white beading thread and secure to back side at top end corner of blue part of flag. String beads in this sequence: four red, two white, four blue, two white, four blue, and eight red. Skipping bottom five red beads, string needle back through remaining beads and go down in top left hole of aida. Pull fringe up close to edge of vinyl aida and run needle and thread through a stitch on back side to secure. Repeat stringing fringe through each hole down left side. Secure and clip thread.

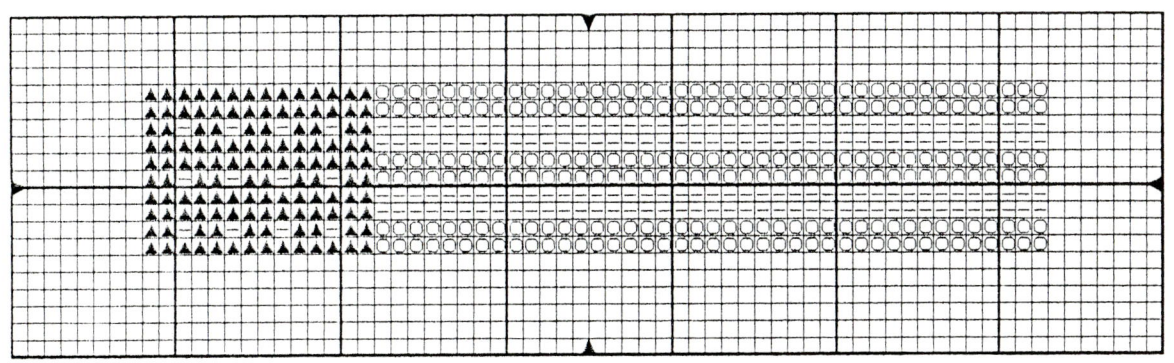

★★ 9 ★★

Liberty Ladybugs

★ Designed by Kelly Hoernig

Catch the spirit with these patriotic painted pins!

You Will Need

For one ladybug
1¾" x 1¾" wood ladybug, ⅛" thick
Acrylic paints*: gray, red, white, blue
Matte varnish*
Star stencil with various sized stars

22-gauge red wire*
Double-ended stylus, fine-grit sandpaper, glue, graphite paper, paintbrushes*, palette paper, paper bag, pin back, round-nose pliers*, sponge

* Used in this project: DecoArt Americana acrylic paints: Payne's Grey, Santa Red, Titanium White, Victorian Blue; varnish • Toner Plastics, Inc. wire • Bond E6000 glue • Loew-Cornell paintbrushes: #4, #14 shader, #1 liner • NSI Wild Wire pliers.

Instructions

1 Sand wood lightly with fine grit sandpaper. Using #14 shader, paint front and sides white. Sand lightly with paper bag. Trace design on with graphite paper.

2 Using #4 shader, paint stripes red, adding a little water. Using #14 shader, float blue along edges and under wings for shadow. Use liner brush to paint white comma stroke on striped body, head, and wings.

3 Paint blue section. Paint stars white, using liner brush or stencil. When dry, use #14 shader to shade stars gray.

4 On ladybug with face, put stylus dot of gray in middle of each eye. Place dot of gray or white at top of each wing in same way.

5 Cut antennae wire to 3". Fold in half and curl ends, using round-nose pliers. Glue antennae and pin back on back of ladybug. Paint front with several coats of varnish.

Beaded Ball Ornament

★ Designed by Carolyn Stearns

Display this ornament any time of the year!

You Will Need

3" frosted glass ball ornament
⅛" double-sided tape*
Double-sided tape stars*
Tiny beads*: blue, red
24" of ½" wide organdy blue ribbon

Craft glue, glass cleaner, paper towel, scissors, small bowl

* Used in this project: ScottiCrafts UltimateBond: Tape; TapeShapes; Teenie Weenie beads.

Instructions

1 Clean ball with glass cleaner. Starting at top of ball, apply first piece of ⅛" tape for vertical stripe. Go to center bottom; cut tape. Apply tape on opposite side. Repeat for eight stripes.

2 Put ball in small bowl to catch beads. Remove tape backing one stripe at a time. Pour red beads over tape and press down gently with fingers.

3 Apply 1" stars in random pattern on ball. Remove tape backing one star at a time and cover with blue beads same as for stripes.

Charms on Safety Pin

★ Designed by Heather McDonald

Make a "charming" pin in a jiffy!

You Will Need

Four round 6mm beads*
Three pewter charms*
Three silver 4mm jump rings*
One silver 1½" safety pin
Round-nose pliers or jewelry-maker's tool*

*Used in this project: THE BEADERY Americana Multi beads, charms, rings, jewelry-maker's tool.

Instructions

1 Use pliers to open jump rings. Attach one to each charm and close jump rings by squeezing them closed with pliers. (Figure 1)

2 If using regular safety pin, use pliers to uncurl loop. String beads and charms onto pin, as shown. Use pliers to re-curl loop in safety pin.

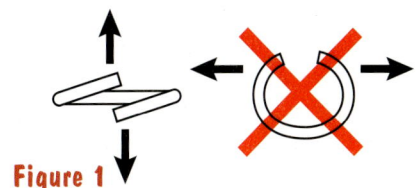

Figure 1

Bead Key Ring

★ Designed by Christine McNeilly

Say it loud and proud with a beaded key ring.

You Will Need

1" split ring
Two pieces of 12" satin cord
Pony beads*: 7 red, 5 white, 3 blue
Alphabet beads*: red G, O, D; white B, L, E, S, S; blue A, M, E, R, I, C, A
Clear drying glue

* Used in this project: THE BEADERY Americana beads.

Instructions

Note: See Stitching Guide on page 25.

1 Attach each cord to ring, using Lark's Head Knot. Line up beads for each strand, as shown.

2 String beads from left to right, with ring on left. Knot end of each cord and dot with glue to secure.

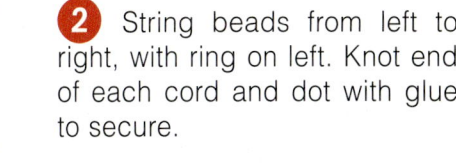

★★ 11 ★★

Rag Basket

★ Designed by Elizabeth Goran

Richly colored Americana fabric strips dress up an ordinary basket filled with decorated papier mâché balls. Use the same fabrics for a one-of-a-kind necklace.

You Will Need

Rag Basket
10½" woven basket
100 assorted 1" x 8" patriotic fabric strips: navy/blue, cranberry/red, ivory/white
1 yd. strong string or twine
Six 1⅞" x ¼" wood stars
Acrylic paint*: navy blue, red
Antiquing gel*: brown, black
Glue gun
Pinking shears, ruler, sand paper, scissors, staple gun

* Used in this project: Darice wood stars • Delta Ceramcoat acrylic paint: Navy Blue, Mendocino Red; antiquing gel.

Candle instructions on page 22

Papier Mâché Balls
One dozen 2½" papier mâché balls
Acrylic paint*: red, navy blue, cream
Antiquing gel*: brown, black
Compressed sponges
Optional: *paint markers, stencils, stickers, stamps, sequins, glitter, etc.*

* Used in this project: Delta Ceramcoat acrylic paint: Mendocino Red, Navy Blue, Buttercream; antiquing gel.

Instructions

Note: See Stitching Guide on page 25.

Rag Basket

❶ Cut string to go around the outer edge of basket, plus 6". Tie a knot in one end of string. Tie fabric strips on string using Larks Head Knots until long enough to go around basket.

❷ Glue string around outer edge of basket with knots facing outward. Slide last fabric strip over knot and glue in place. Trim all fabric strip ends with pinking shears, varying lengths slightly.

❸ Paint three stars with two coats of red and three stars with navy blue. When stars are dry, sand edges slightly for an aged look. Mix a little black antiquing gel into the brown. Brush onto stars and then wipe off with clean cloth. Space stars evenly around edge of basket and glue onto fabric strips.

Papier Mâché Balls

1 Paint balls with several coats of paint to cover thoroughly.

2 Mix a little black antiquing gel with brown. Paint ball with a brush. Wipe off with clean cloth.

Decorating Options

★ Cut stars or hearts from compressed sponges. Dip sponges in water and squeeze out. Dip sponges in paint, tap off on paper, and press onto painted balls.

★ Draw lines and shapes with glue and shake glitter onto the wet glue.

★ Use stencils to make patriotic designs.

★ Use rubber stamps to stamp patriotic images on balls.

★ Glue star-shaped sequins on balls.

★ Write patriotic words with paint markers in a spiral around balls.

★ Use sponge to tap color onto surface.

★ Dip end of paintbrush into paint and make dots all over surface.

Rag Necklace

You Will Need

1 yd. navy cotton cording
Forty 1″ x 4″ strips of assorted patriotic fabrics
Three ¼″ x 1⅞″ wood stars
Two gold 20mm bells
Acrylic paint: navy blue, cream, gold
Navy embroidery floss
Paintbrush, pinking shears, sponge, staple gun

* Used in this project: Darice stars • Delta Ceramcoat acrylic paint: Navy Blue, Buttercream; Gleams Metallic Kim Gold.

Instructions

1 Paint front and back of stars with two coats cream. When dry, lightly sponge gold on front of stars. Paint sides and outline front of stars with gold. Paint words on stars with navy.

2 Staple one fabric strip to center back of each star. Tie star around center of cording in a knot. Tie remaining stars 2″ to left and right of center star. With embroidery floss, tie two bells centered between stars. Tie fabric strips between stars and bells.

3 Trim fabric ends shorter with the pinking shears. Fluff fabric with fingers to add fullness. Knot cording to desired length for necklace. Dip ends of cording into glue to keep from unraveling.

What If You . . .

Drape it as a swag on a mantel or wall.

USA Arch

★ Designed by Molieve Null

This simple arch will look great hanging in your window or from a light fixture.

You Will Need

12" x 2½" x 1" white foam floral wreath*
Four 1" x 4" white foam star shapes*
12" x 36" x ½" thick white foam sheet*
Acrylic paint*: red, blue, gold metallic
Wire*: 3 yds. of 18-gauge red; 6" of 26-gauge gold
Filament line, glue*, metal nail file or serrated knife, paper, pencil, small flat brush, straight pins

* Used in this project: FloraCraft wreath • DecoArt Americana acrylic paint: True Red, Primary Blue, Emperor's Gold metallic • NSI wire • Crafter's Pick glue • Styrofoam Brand foam stars, sheet.

- To better fill surface when painting foam, add small amount of glue to paint and thin slightly with water. Mix well, then paint.
- For smooth cut, make small slits ⅛" outside line of letters with point of tool. Then cut all the way through.

Instructions

1 For arch, cut wreath in half. Twist 6" length of gold wire into small eye shape with bent ends. (Figure 1) Glue ends on back top center of one arch. Glue backs of two arches together to form rounded arch.

2 Trace letter patterns on paper and cut out. Pin patterns on foam sheet. Cut two of each letter from foam, using metal nail file or serrated knife. Rub to remove any loose particles. Use small flat brush to paint each letter with red. Paint edges with gold metallic, letting some red show through gold. Let dry. Paint one side only of each star with blue. Let dry.

3 Glue letters and stars onto arch, one side at a time. Allow glue to dry completely before repeating on other side of arch.

4 Cut fourteen 7" lengths of wire. Curl wire around a pencil. Glue one end and insert wire into letters, stars, and arch, as shown. Uncurl wires slightly on stars and arch.

5 Thread filament line through gold wire hanger.

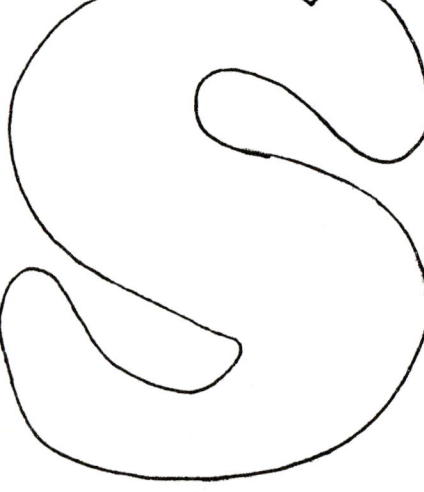

Edge of arch
Gold wire hanger
Figure 1

Sponged Tie

★ Designed by Gail Green

Sponge paint simple stars in a pattern on a plain white tie.

You Will Need

Star sponges*: 2″, ¾″
Fabric paint*: blue, red
White silk tie
Foam plate, scrap paper, sponge brush or wedge

*Used in this project: Plaid Enterprises sponges; Decorative Glaze: Pompeii Red (#53038), Nantucket Blue (#53025) • Janlynn/Arty's silk tie.

- Before beginning project, practice stamping on scrap paper or fabric. Apply paint evenly.
- If desired, embellish red stars: glue on a button; outline with dimensional fabric paint; or cover images with a thin layer of fabric glue and add glitter.

Instructions

1 Protect work surface. Place tie right side up, with large bottom section of tie closest to you. Insert scrap paper beneath entire length of tie.

2 Squeeze half-dollar size circle of blue paint onto plate. Spread paint flat with sponge brush. Press smallest star in blue paint. Stamp image in lower left corner of tie. Repeat to stamp diagonal row of blue stars to the right. Stamp blue stars in diagonal row to the left. Continue zigzag star pattern to other end of tie.

3 Squeeze red paint onto plate and spread out. Stamp single red stars in open areas, using medium-sized star stamp.

PAINTED SWEATSHIRT STARS
page 17

Cut 6 of small star
Cut 1 each of 4 larger stars

Patriotic Beret

★ Designed by Ellen Allan

Top off any patriotic outfit with a fashionable felt beret.

You Will Need

½ yd. wool felt*: red, blue, white
Red thread
Clean wire dog brush, fabric scissors, pencil, sewing machine with straight and zigzag stitches, sewing machine needle size 9 or 11, steam iron, straight pins, tracing paper.

* Used in this project: National Nonwovens felt.

Note: Enlarge patterns 200%.

BERET

Cut 1 blue felt
Cut 1 red felt

fold

Instructions

1 Trace and cut out circle and star patterns. Cut one FULL circle from red felt and one from blue felt. Cut center out of red circle. Cut one white star from white felt.

2 For hatband, turn inside circle edge ⅜" to inside and straight stitch down ¼" from edge. Fit on head. If you need to make it bigger, gently pull to size.

3 Center and pin star on navy circle. Using zigzag set on a medium width and buttonhole length, stitch star down. Use clean wire dog brush to brush right sides of both pieces to make soft and hairy. Do not over brush. Press from wrong side to shape, if necessary.

4 With right sides together, stitch red and blue circles using ½" seam allowance around outside edges. Trim seam allowance to ¼". Finger-press seam open. Topstitch ⅛" from both sides of seam. Use steam iron to flatten seam, then fluff with dog brush, if necessary.

BERET STAR

Cut 1
white felt

fold

Painted Sweatshirt

★ Designed by Billie Worrell

Decorate an easy-to-paint sweatshirt using stencils, patterns, and tape for guides.

You Will Need

White sweatshirt, 100- or 50/50-percent polyester
Textile medium*
Acrylic paints*: blue, red, white
Fabric brushes and liner*
1" wide low-tack masking tape
Cardboard to fit inside shirt, Con-Tact (adhesive-back paper), iron, palette, palette knife, paper towels, press cloth, ruler, scissors, sharp craft knife, stencil or cosmetic sponge, tracing paper, water container

* Used in this project: Delta textile medium; Ceramcoat acrylic paint: Opaque Blue, Opaque Red, White; paintbrushes: Nos. 16, 14, 10 shaders, No. 6 round, No. 1 liner.

Note: Trace and cut out star patterns on page 15.
The pattern and instructions are for an extra-large sweatshirt. Adjust to size of shirt used.

Instructions

1 Wash, dry, and press shirt. Do not use fabric softener. Place cardboard inside shirt.

2 Trace #1 smallest star onto adhesive paper six times and cut out (positive pattern). Trace #2 - #5 larger stars on adhesive-back paper and cut out with craft knife, leaving ample space between each star (negative pattern). Trace wording onto tracing paper.

3 For blue yoke, measure 6½" long x 7" wide rectangle, starting at shoulders. Tape off with masking tape for straight lines. Remove backing from #1 stars and stick on this section. This will block off paint as you work. Squeeze blue paint and textile medium onto palette using equal portions. Mix well using palette knife. Use No. 16 shader brush and fill in this area, directly over stars. Remove stars and tape.

4 Tape five 7" strips vertically below blue area. Tape addition piece horizontally under vertical strips to keep ends straight. Mix red paint and textile medium together and paint the open strips using No. 14 shader. Remove tape.

5 Use transfer paper and transfer wording on top of red stripes. Use round brush and blue mix to paint letters. Mix white with textile medium and highlight tops and left side of letters with No. 10 shader. Do this while blue paint is still wet. Use liner brush to clean up any edges.

6 Remove adhesive backing from #2 - #5 stars and place on shirt as desired. Stencil stars using sponge and blue and red mixes of paint.

7 Heat-set shirt using a damp press cloth for 20 seconds. Allow five days before laundering to give the paint curing time. Machine or line dry.

Star Yard Pokes

★ **Designed by Kerry Liebner**

Glittery stars will brighten your yard!

You Will Need

Large *for one star*

Acrylic paint*: red, white, blue
Metallic paint*: gold
Clear acrylic spray sealer
22″ of ¼″ wood dowel
9″ diameter wood star
Glitter: red, white, blue
2 yds. of ¼″ wide white ribbon
2 yds. of ⅛″ wide ribbon: red, blue
Drill with ¼″ bit, glue, paintbrush, paper plate (palette), water

* Used in this project: Delta Ceramcoat acrylic paint: Napthol Red Light, White, Opaque Blue; Gleams Metallic Kim Gold; sealer • Loew-Cornell #6 flat brush • Crafter's Pick glue.

Small *for one star*

Gold acrylic paint*
Star template*
#6 flat brush*
¼″ white craft foam
13″ length of 3/16″ wood dowel
32″ of silver wired ribbon or chenille stem
Glitter: red, white, blue
Glue*, pencil, scissors or craft knife

* Used in this project: Plaid FolkArt Metallics: Inca Gold; Simply Stencils Star Template • Loew-Cornell # 6 flat brush • Crafter's Pick glue.

Enlarge to any size desired (large 9″ and small 5″ stars are shown).

Instructions

Large

1 Drill hole in base of star for dowel, ½″ deep. Paint star with red, white, or blue. Paint dowel gold.

2 With brush or finger, apply thin layer of glue on front of star. Sprinkle star with glitter. Glue and insert dowel into star. Spray star and dowel with sealer.

3 Cut ribbons to 1 yard lengths. Tie ribbons together in a bow. Glue bow at base of star.

Small

1 Trace star pattern onto craft foam. Cut star shape from foam with scissors. Cut slit in base of star with knife to insert dowel.

2 With brush or finger, apply thin layer of glue on front of star. Sprinkle star with glitter. Using flat brush, paint dowel gold. Glue and insert dowel into star.

3 Cut ribbon into two 16″ lengths. Fold each ribbon in half. Curl ribbon around a pencil. Glue fold of each ribbon at base of star.

Stained Glass Candles

★ Designed by Dorothy Egan

Turn simple jars into stunning candles!

You Will Need

All Jars
Small mouth quart canning jar
2½" clear glass flowerpot
Votive candle, white or red
18" length of patriotic ribbon
Treasure Gold (Classic)*
Gallery Glass*
  Window Color: Ruby Red, Royal Blue, White Pearl
  One package Instant Lead Lines
  One package Thin Redi-Lead
Flexible ruler, glue*, paintbrushes ½" and #4 flat, soft cloth, straight pins, craft knife

Individual Jars
Gallery Glass Bevels Mold*
Nine 22mm acrylic rhinestone stars
Two Miniature flags
Sparkle floral pick
14" of blue foil star garland

* Used in this project: Plaid Gallery Glass: paints, leading, molds • Bond E-6000 glue.

• For gold look on black Redi-Lead, use soft cloth to apply Treasure Gold before removing lead from paper backing.
• Paint one side of jar at a time. Lay jar flat to dry before painting next side.

Instructions

All Jars

❶ Use soft cloth to apply Treasure Gold on Redi-Lead strips.

❷ Peel Redi-Lead strips from paper backing. Apply strip around neck of jar. Apply strip around jar along bottom edge.

❸ Place vertical strips along two seam lines of jar. Trim away excess lead with knife. Apply two more strips equal distance between first two, dividing jar into equal quarters.

❹ When jar is completed, tie ribbon around neck of jar. Trim ends at a slant or in a "v." Glue trims on ribbon. Place flowerpot in neck of jar. Put votive candle in flowerpot

Jar #1

❶ Apply horizontal strip around jar approximately 2½" below top strip.

❷ On lower section of jar add 1" stripes 1" wide. Fill in strips alternately with Ruby Red and White Pearl.

❸ Glue two stars in each of top quarters. Squeeze Royal Blue Window Color to fill in around stars.

Jar #2

❶ Apply two more strips on each quarter section, making 1" wide stripes. Use thin leading strips to create wavy lines in alternate stripe.

❷ Squeeze paint directly from tube to fill in stripes with Window Color. Fill plain stripes with Royal Blue. Fill stripes with wavy lines, using White Pearl and Ruby Red.

Jar #3

❶ Use Ruby Red or Royal Blue to fill large oval design in bevels mold. When dry, remove design from mold and set aside.

❷ Paint back of design with very thin coat of same color. Center design in quarter section and press firmly. Use thin leading strips to outline design. See photo for placement of other strips radiating out from oval. Fill in outer sections, alternating red and white around blue ovals and blue and white around red ovals.

Uncle Sam Doll

★ Designed by Chris Malone

Make a roly-poly Uncle Sam to carry our nation's message of unity.

Finished size: 7½" tall

You Will Need

- 4" white foam ball*
- 2" wood ball knob (head)
- Two ¾" wood ball knobs (hands)
- ⅜" wood ball (nose)
- Three 1⅞" wood stars
- ¼ yd. fabric, blue and gold print
- ⅓ yd. fabric, red and white print
- 6" chenille stem
- 13½ ft. white bumpy doll hair yarn
- 7½" long forked branch
- 2" plastic film canister
- 3" square lightweight cardboard
- 9" piece of ⅝" wide gold grosgrain ribbon
- Small amount polyester fiberfill
- Acrylic paints: base flesh, shading flesh, black, white, gold
- Permanent fine-tip black marking pen
- Spray matte finish
- Strong thread (carpet, buttonhole)
- Sewing thread: red, white
- Fabric glue, glue gun and glue sticks, knife, iron, needle, paint brush, paper towel, pencil, ruler, sandpaper, scissors, small stencil brush, straight pins, stylus or toothpick, (optional) sewing machine

* Used in this project: STYROFOAM Brand foam ball.

Shirt
*Tape 4 pattern pieces together BEFORE cutting from fabric
Cut 1
red print

Instructions

1 Shirt and Pants patterns are only ¼ of pattern needed. Tape four pieces together along straight edges BEFORE cutting patterns from fabric.

2 To sew shirt and pants together, divide outer edge of pants and inner edge of shirt into fourths; mark with pins. Matching markers, pin circles together, right sides facing. Sew with ¼" seam. Use strong thread to sew gathering stitches around outer edge of shirt. Use knife to cut small slice off 4" foam ball. Place flat side of ball on center wrong side of blue circle. Pull thread to gather tightly at top of ball. Knot and clip thread.

3 For nose, rub ⅜" wood ball over sandpaper to make flat area for gluing. Glue ball on center of one side of 2" head ball. Paint head and ¾" hand balls base flesh and stars gold. For cheeks, dip stencil brush into shading flesh; remove excess paint on paper towel. Tap brush on each side of nose. For eyes, dip stylus into black paint and touch on face. Make several white highlight dots on each cheek. Use pen to write "united," "we," and "stand" on stars. Use stylus and black paint to make dots on letters. Draw eyebrows on face and stitch lines around each star with pen. Spray all painted pieces with two light coats of matte finish.

4 For arms, cut chenille stem in half. Glue one end of each piece in each hand ball. For sleeves cut two 3¼" x 4¾" rectangles from red print. Fold each in half, right sides facing, and sew ¼" seam along 3¼" side to make a tube. Press in ¼" hem on one end of each sleeve. Use red thread to sew gathering stitches through hem end. Insert hand and pull thread to gather sleeve around base of knob; knot and clip thread. Use small dots of glue to hold sleeve in place. Lightly stuff each sleeve with fiberfill. Fold two pleats at top of each sleeve and tack or glue to hold. Glue pleated end of arms on top of ball on opposite sides. Glue head on top of body.

5 Cut yarn into three 4-foot lengths and one 18″ length. For beard, wrap one long piece around four fingers held together. Remove from hand and tie center of bundle with white thread. Repeat to make two more bundles. For mustache, wrap 18″ piece around two fingers and tie same as for beard. Glue center of three larger bundles along bottom of face, close together. Glue small bundle under nose.

6 For hat crown, place top of canister on wrong side of blue fabric and draw around it; cut out circle ¼″ from line. Apply glue sparingly around side of canister at top edge. Place fabric circle on top of canister and press edges down over glue.

Cut 2½″ x 4½″ rectangle from blue fabric. Press under ¼″ hem on one long edge of rectangle. Glue fabric around canister, with hem edge at top; overlap and glue ends on back.

7 For hat brim, use pattern to cut cardboard base. Mark pattern on wrong side of blue fabric two times, leaving ½″ between circles. Cut one out on lines. Cut second one out ¼″ larger on outer circle. Glue larger ring to one side of cardboard; turn edges over to back side of cardboard and glue down. Glue smaller ring on back of cardboard, covering fabric edges.

Apply glue to inner edge of brim; cover with crown. For hatband, cut 1¼″ x 4½″ strip from red print. Press both long edges into center of wrong side of band. Wrap band around base of crown, overlapping ends in back.

8 Glue hat on top of head. Tie ribbon in bow; trim ends in a "v." Glue bow on side of hat. Glue stars on forks of branch. Bend one arm around branch and glue to hold. Glue branch on body to stabilize doll.

Hat Brim
Cut 1 cardboard
1 blue print

Pants
*Tape 4 pattern pieces together BEFORE cutting from fabric
Cut 1 blue print

Old Glory Bouquet

★ Designed by Kelley Taylor

Create a simple arrangement in minutes!

You Will Need

6⅜″ tall cobalt blue vase
Ten red silk tulips
Five 4″ x 6″ American flags
Marbles, pebbles, or sand
Wire cutters

Instructions

1 Fill base of vase with marbles for weight and to hold flags and flowers.

2 Cut stems of flowers with wire cutters to desired height. Place five flags in vase, spacing them evenly with extra space open in front. Insert one flower in each space between two flags, inserting three in front space. Insert several tulips in center of vase.

HURON PUBLIC LIBRARY
333 WILLIAMS STREET
HURON, OHIO 44839

★★ 21 ★★

Paper Doll Candle

★ Designed by Koren Russell

United we stand, hand to hand. Cutout dolls convey the message clearly tied around a unity candle.

You Will Need

9½" x 3" strip of gesso primed canvas
Acrylic paint*: burgundy, blue, beige
Crackle medium*
Gold metallic paint*
Gold paint marker*
Embroidery floss: gold metallic
3½" x 4" oval or 3" pillar candle
Embroidery needle, paintbrushes, paper towel, pencil, ruler, scissors

* Used in this project: DecoArt Americana acrylic paint: Deep Burgundy, Admiral Blue, Toffee; Perfect Crackle; Dazzling Metallics paint: Glorious Gold;
• ZIG Painty marker.

Instructions

❶ Fold canvas to cut a multiple-doll chain or trace pattern one at a time on canvas, connecting hands and feet, for a total of six figures.

❷ Lightly pencil line 1¼" down from the top of second, fourth, and sixth figures. Draw horizontal lines, ¼" apart, below line. Paint top section of striped figures blue. Paint all of first, third, and fifth figures blue. Paint second, fourth, and last stripe burgundy. Paint remaining stripes beige. Randomly paint stars in blue sections of striped figures.

❸ When paint has dried, apply three coats of Perfect Crackle Step 1. Let dry. Apply coat of Perfect Crackle Step 2. Let dry.

❹ Mix equal amounts of gold paint and water. Paint mixture on a figure. Wipe off paint so gold remains only in cracks. Repeat with other figures. Use gold marker to outline figures and stripes. Run marker along edges of figures.

❺ Stitch hands on ends together with three strands of floss; do not knot thread. Repeat for feet. Slide ring over candle. Pull floss ends until figures are tight against candle. Tie square knots, and trim ends to ¼" lengths.

❻ Wrap floss around candle near top three times. Tie square knot and trim ends. Repeat on bottom of candle.

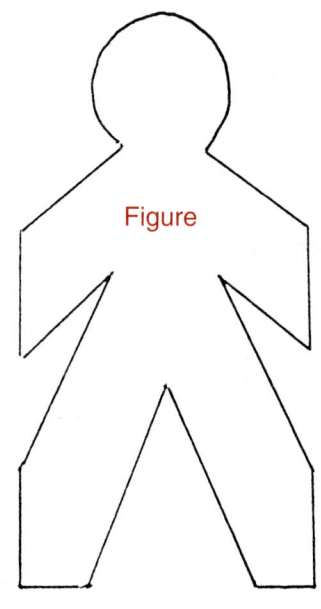

Figure

★★ 22 ★★

Stamp Magnets

★ Designed by Mary Lynn Maloney

Turn patriotic postage stamps into pins that look like tiny, framed works of art.

You Will Need

U.S. postage stamps with flag or statue of liberty images
Cardstock
Decorative paper
Mat board
Cancellation marks rubber stamp*
Sienna ink*
Decorative scissors*: stamp; deckle
⅛" thick self-adhesive dimensional dots*
½" wide self-adhesive magnet strips*
Metallic braid: red, gold, silver
Craft knife, glue stick, metal edge ruler, pencil, scissors, self-healing cutting board with measuring guidelines

* Used in these projects: Stampa Rosa, Inc. rubber stamp, dimensional dots • Magnetic Specialty, Inc. magnets • Clearsnap, Inc. ink • Fiskars scissors.

Instructions

1 Affix stamp(s) on piece of cardstock. Using ruler, craft knife, and cutting board, trim cardstock so that small border frames stamp. **Option:** *Cut edge using decorative scissors.* Stamp cancel marks across piece or wait until magnet is assembled.

2 Lay stamp piece onto mat board. Determine how much of a mat border you want around postage stamp piece and mark mat board with pencil. Cut mat board to desired size.

3 Choose piece of decorative paper that contrasts with cardstock. Trim paper so that ½" to ¾" extends beyond sides of mat board. Cover wrong side of decorative paper with thick layer of glue. Lay mat board onto center of glued paper. Cut corners of paper on diagonal to reduce bulk and wrap paper around to back of mat board. To finish back, cut decorative paper rectangle to cover unfinished area on back and glue in place.

4 Option: *Punch a small hole on each side of stamp piece. Insert several metallic braids into hole, front to back. Glue ends on back.* Affix four to five self-adhesive dimensional dots on back of stamp piece. Center and glue this piece on front of paper-covered mat board. **Option:** *Tie several pieces of metallic braid around one side of piece.* Cut piece of magnet strip to fit and glue on center back of mat.

Safety Pin Jewelry

★ Designed by Samantha McNesby

Quick and easy to make, these safety pin projects make a bold statement!

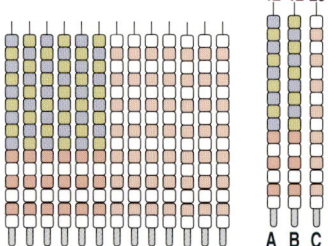

Figure 1   **Figure 2**

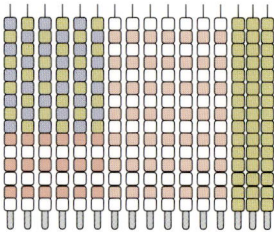

Figure 3 (repeat 4 times)

You Will Need

Flag Pin

Fourteen size 2 (1½″) silver safety pins*

Size 10/0 seed beads*: red, white, blue, metallic gold

Kitchen knife or metal nail file, needle-nose pliers

* Used in this project: Darice safety pins • Bead it by Nicole seed beads.

Flag Bracelet

Sixty-four size 2 (1½″) silver safety pins*

Size 10/0 seed beads: red, white, blue, metallic gold

1 yd. white elastic cord*

Kitchen knife, masking tape

* Used in this project: Rhode Island Textile Company Stretchrite elastic beading cord.

Instructions

Flag Pin

1 (Figure 1) Follow pattern to string seed beads onto thirteen pins. Open pins, string beads, and close pins.

Use point of kitchen knife to unbend loop at base of remaining pin. To add beaded pins, start from far left of pattern. Thread looped base of beaded pin onto open point and work it around loop. It should hang with beads facing front. Follow pattern to string all beaded pins. Use pliers to bend pin back into shape.

Flag Bracelet

1 (Figure 2) Follow pattern to string seed beads onto 64 pins, same as for Flag Pin: 12 A, 12 B, 28 C, 12 D. Open pin, string beads, and close pin. Slide each beaded pin onto flat blade of knife as you work; this will help you keep your place in pattern as you work.

2 Cut two 18″ lengths of elastic cord. Tape one end of each length of cord to flat surface 1″ apart, leaving a 6″ tail. (Figure 3) Start at far left of pattern and string beaded pins onto elastic cords. Insert cords through loop at base of pin and through hole in pin clasp. The beads making up "flag" portion of bracelet should be strung with clasp side down. The "gold" portion of bracelet should be strung with clasp side up. Repeat pattern four times to string all beaded pins. Remove tape from end of elastic cords and tie top cords together in a square knot. Tie bottom cords together in same way. Trim tails.

Acknowledgments

Graphic Designer
Marilyn Hochstatter

Photographer
Ross Hubbard

The following Society of Craft Designers members also donated projects for the book but space did not permit their inclusion:

Lucy Ashton
Betty Auth
Ginny Baker
Kim Ballor
Marianna Bellantoni
Denise Bielick
Nancy Billetdeaux
Karen Blonigen
Faun Bonewits
Karen Booth
Ann Butler
Reba Campbell
Nikki Carvey
Barb Chauncey
Sherry Coupland
Carol Dace
Sharon Dugas
Betsy Edwards
Jill Evans
Sally Evans
Fran Farris
Maria Filosa
Diane Flowers
Leslie Frederick
Melinda Frewin
Lisa Galvin
Jacqueline Gikow
Denise Giles
Doris Glovier
Cindy Groom Harry
Sherry Harrington
Debba Haupert
Monica Heeren
Nancy Hoerner
Mimi Huszer Fagnant
Lorraine Kazan
Sandy Kinnamon
Carol Krob
Sandy Laipply
Kerry Liebner
Arline Lowenthal
Susan Lowenthal
Susan Lowman
Julie MacGuffee
Lorine Mason
Connie Matricardi
Carol Melnick
Ginger Miller
Jan Monahan
Sylvia Montroy
Beverly Morgan
Tammy Muto
Debra Quartermain
Barbara Quast
Helen Rafson
Joanna Randolph Rott
Cindy Rippe
Gail Ritchey
Andrea Rothenberg
Delores Ruzicka
Phyllis Sandford
Connie Sanford
Vicki Schreiner
Rebecca Stearns
Jon-Michael Vasek
Kathy Wirth
Linda Wyszynski
Madonna Yashinski
Deborah Zeisloft

Stitching Guide

Cross-Stitch

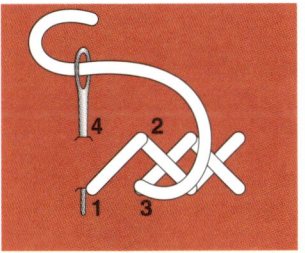

Overcast Stitch

Reverse Continental Stitch

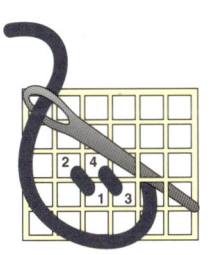

Whip Stitch

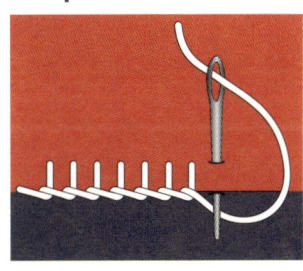

French Knot

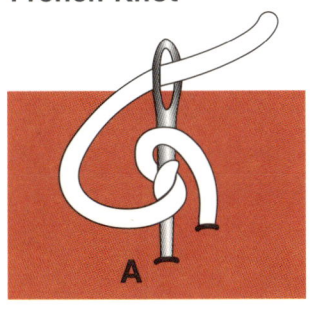

Lark's Head Knot

Fold cord in half, place fold over ring, and bring loop down behind ring. Insert cord ends through loop and pull cords to tighten.

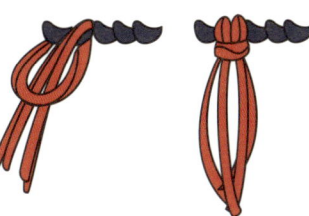

Display Your National Pride!

Filled with quick and easy designs, this is a resource you will turn to again and again for inspiring projects.

This unique compilation includes:

★ More than 25 projects, from candles and baskets to pins, bracelets, and garments

★ Projects for the entire family

★ Clear step-by-step instructions with helpful illustrations

Enjoy making projects that show you are proud to be an American!

★ ★ ★

A portion of the proceeds from the sale of this book will be donated to the American Red Cross. Do your part to support a worthwhile charity!

Krause Publications

ISBN 0-87349-444-X $7.95